The Ultimate Hot Chocolate Recipe Book

Recipe Book

Discover A Wide Variety of Delicious Hot Chocolate Recipes!

BY: Valeria Ray

License Notes

Copyright © 2020 Valeria Ray All Rights Reserved

All rights to the content of this book are reserved by the Author without exception unless permission is given stating otherwise.

The Author have no claims as to the authenticity of the content and the Reader bears all responsibility and risk when following the content. The Author is not liable for any reparations, damages, accidents, injuries or other incidents occurring from the Reader following all or part of this publication.

Table of Contents

Introduction 6

1. Classic Hot Chocolate 7

2. Nutella Hot Chocolate 9

3. Biscoff Hot Chocolate 11

4. Peanut Butter Hot Chocolate 13

5. Mocha Hot Chocolate 15

6. White Hot Chocolate 17

7. Nutella Mocha Hot Chocolate 19

8. White Peppermint Hot Chocolate 21

9. Mexican Hot Chocolate 23

10. Orange Hot Chocolate 25

11. Red Velvet Hot Chocolate 27

12. Lavender Hot Chocolate 29

13. Almond Butter Hot Chocolate 31

14. Coconut Hot Chocolate 33

15. Candy Cane Hot Chocolate 35

16. KitKat Hot Chocolate 37

17. Sea Salt Hot Chocolate 39

18. Cinnamon Hot Chocolate 41

19. White Mocha Hot Chocolate 43

20. Peanut Butter Mocha Hot Chocolate 45

21. White Matcha Hot Chocolate 47

22. Double Chocolate Hot Chocolate 49

23. Gingerbread Hot Chocolate 51

24. Pumpkin Spice Hot Chocolate 53

25. KitKat Mocha Hot Chocolate 55

26. Orange Mocha Hot Chocolate 57

27. Vegan Hot Chocolate 59

28. Caramel Hot Chocolate 61

29. Keto Hot Chocolate 63

30. Lavender White Hot Chocolate 65

Conclusion 67

About the Author 68

Author's Afterthoughts 69

Introduction

If you are on the hunt for delicious & decadent hot chocolate recipes that can carry you through winter, look no further than this recipe book! Filled with all kinds of variations on hot chocolate, this book is perfect for all kinds of taste buds!

What is more, all the recipes in the book are easy and come together in less than 10 minutes! Plus, all of them have detailed instructions that make them easy for everybody! So, what are you waiting for? Choose a recipe and let us get started!

1. Classic Hot Chocolate

Hot, rich and creamy, this drink is the equivalent of coziness in a mug.

Makes: 4 servings

Prep: 5 mins

Cook: 5 mins

Ingredients:

- 2 cups milk, divided
- 1 cup heavy cream
- 1 ½ tsp. cornstarch
- 6 oz. semi-sweet chocolate

Directions:

In a large saucepan, combine 1 ½ cups milk and cream.

Next, in a small bowl, whisk together remaining milk and cornstarch until well combined. Add it to the pan and whisk again.

Cook on medium low for about 4 minutes or until bubbles start to appear around the edge. Remove, add in the chocolate chips and whisk until well combined.

Lastly, divide between mugs and serve.

2. Nutella Hot Chocolate

This is a delicious hot chocolate that Nutella lovers will absolutely love!

Makes: 4 servings

Prep: 5 mins

Cook: 5 mins

Ingredients:

- 2 cups milk, divided
- 1 cup heavy cream
- 1 ½ tsp. cornstarch
- 2 oz. semi-sweet chocolate
- 2 tbsp. Nutella

Directions:

In a saucepan, combine 1 ½ cups milk and cream.

Next, in a small bowl, whisk together remaining milk and cornstarch until well combined. Add it to the pan and whisk again.

Cook on medium low for about 4 minutes or until bubbles start to appear around the edge. Remove, add in the chocolate chips and Nutella and whisk until well combined.

Lastly, divide between mugs and serve.

3. Biscoff Hot Chocolate

A creamy and smooth Lotus Biscoff hot chocolate recipe.

Makes: 4 servings

Prep: 5 mins

Cook: 5 mins

Ingredients:

- 2 cups milk, divided
- 1 tbsp. chocolate syrup
- 2 tbsp. Lotus Biscoff
- Whipped cream

Directions:

In a pan, add the milk & heat until almost boiling. Add in the chocolate syrup and Lotus Biscoff spread and mix till combined. Serve in mugs and add whipped cream on top.

4. Peanut Butter Hot Chocolate

Undoubtedly, this is perfect for anyone who loves peanut butter!

Makes: 4 servings

Prep: 5 mins

Cook: 5 mins

Ingredients:

- 2 cups milk, divided
- 1 tbsp. chocolate syrup
- 2 tbsp. peanut butter

Directions:

In a saucepan, add the milk & heat until almost boiling. Add in the chocolate syrup and peanut butter and mix till combined. Serve in mugs and add whipped cream on top.

5. Mocha Hot Chocolate

A hot chocolate recipe with coffee!

Makes: 4 servings

Prep: 5 mins

Cook: 5 mins

Ingredients:

- 2 cups milk, divided
- 1 cup heavy cream
- 1 ½ tsp. cornstarch
- 6 oz. semi-sweet chocolate
- 2 tsp. instant coffee powder

Directions:

In a large saucepan, combine 1 ½ cups milk and cream. In a small bowl, whisk together remaining milk and cornstarch until well combined. Add it to the pan and whisk again.

Cook on medium low for about 4 minutes or until bubbles start to appear around the edge. Remove, add in the chocolate chips and coffee powder and whisk until well combined.

Divide between mugs and serve.

6. White Hot Chocolate

Switch up your usual hot chocolate with this white chocolate version!

Makes: 4 servings

Prep: 5 mins

Cook: 5 mins

Ingredients:

- 2 cups milk, divided
- 1 cup heavy cream
- 1 ½ tsp. cornstarch
- 6 oz. white chocolate
- 1 ½ tsp. vanilla extract

Directions:

In a large saucepan, combine 1 ½ cups milk and cream.

Next, in a small bowl, whisk together remaining milk and cornstarch until well combined. Add it to the pan and whisk again.

Cook on medium low for about 4 minutes or until bubbles start to appear around the edge. Remove, add in the chocolate and vanilla and whisk until well combined.

Lastly, divide between mugs and serve.

7. Nutella Mocha Hot Chocolate

Delicious hot chocolate with Nutella and coffee!

Makes: 4 servings

Prep: 5 mins

Cook: 5 mins

Ingredients:

- 2 cups milk, divided
- 1 cup heavy cream
- 1 ½ tsp. cornstarch
- 2 oz. semi-sweet chocolate
- 2 tbsp. Nutella
- 2 tsp. coffee powder

Directions:

In a saucepan, combine 1 ½ cups milk and cream. In a small bowl, whisk together remaining milk and cornstarch until well combined. Add it to the pan and whisk again.

Cook on medium low for about 4 minutes or until bubbles start to appear around the edge. Remove, add in the chocolate chips, Nutella and coffee powder and whisk until well combined.

Divide between mugs and serve.

8. White Peppermint Hot Chocolate

This is an amazing hot chocolate to have around holidays.

Makes: 4 servings

Prep: 5 mins

Cook: 5 mins

Ingredients:

- 2 cups milk, divided
- 1 cup heavy cream
- 1 ½ tsp. cornstarch
- 6 oz. white chocolate
- 1 tsp. vanilla extract
- 1 tsp. peppermint extract

Directions:

In a large saucepan, combine 1 ½ cups milk and cream.

Next, in a small bowl, whisk together remaining milk and cornstarch until well combined. Add it to the pan and whisk again.

Cook on medium low for about 4 minutes or until bubbles start to appear around the edge. Remove, add in the chocolate and vanilla and whisk until well combined.

Lastly, divide between mugs and serve.

9. Mexican Hot Chocolate

This hot chocolate has a hint of spice to it and is absolutely delicious!

Makes: 4 servings

Prep: 5 mins

Cook: 5 mins

Ingredients:

- 3 cups milk, divided
- 1 ½ tsp. cornstarch
- ½ tbsp. vanilla
- 2 tsp. cinnamon
- ½ tsp. ground nutmeg
- 6 oz. semi-sweet chocolate

Directions:

In a saucepan, combine 2 ½ cups milk. In a bowl, whisk together remaining milk & cornstarch until well combined. Add it to the pan and whisk again. Add in the spices and vanilla.

Cook on medium low for about 4 minutes or until bubbles start to appear around the edge. Remove, add in the chocolate chips and whisk until well combined.

Divide between mugs and serve.

10. Orange Hot Chocolate

A classic combination in a hot chocolate form!

Makes: 4 servings

Prep: 5 mins

Cook: 5 mins

Ingredients:

- 2 cups milk, divided
- 1 cup heavy cream
- 1 ½ tsp. cornstarch
- Rind of an orange
- 6 oz. semi-sweet chocolate

Directions:

In a large saucepan, combine 1 ½ cups milk, cream and the rind.

Next, in a small bowl, whisk together remaining milk and cornstarch until well combined. Add it to the pan and whisk again.

Cook on medium low for about 4 minutes or until bubbles start to appear around the edge. Remove and take out the rind. Add in the chocolate chips and whisk until well combined.

Lastly, divide between mugs and serve.

11. Red Velvet Hot Chocolate

Delicious red velvet hot chocolate for red velvet lovers!

Makes: 4 servings

Prep: 5 mins

Cook: 5 mins

Ingredients:

- 2 cups milk, divided
- 1 cup heavy cream
- 1 ½ tsp. cornstarch
- 6 oz. white chocolate
- 1 ½ tsp. vanilla extract
- Red food color, as needed

Directions:

In a large saucepan, combine 1 ½ cups milk and cream.

Next, in a small bowl, whisk together remaining milk and cornstarch until well combined. Add it to the pan and whisk again.

Cook on medium low for about 4 minutes or until bubbles start to appear around the edge. Remove, add in the chocolate and vanilla and whisk until well combined. Add in the red food color as needed.

Lastly, divide between mugs and serve.

12. Lavender Hot Chocolate

This hot chocolate has a hint of floral sweetness from the lavender.

Makes: 4 servings

Prep: 5 mins

Cook: 5 mins

Ingredients:

- 2 cups milk, divided
- 1 cup heavy cream
- 1 ½ tsp. cornstarch
- 1 tbsp. dried lavender
- 6 oz. semi-sweet chocolate

Directions:

In a large saucepan, combine 1 ½ cups milk, cream and lavender.

Next, cook for about 5 mins then remove from heat and let it steep for 10 mins. Strain mixture into a bowl and put it back into the pan.

In a small bowl, whisk together remaining milk and cornstarch until well combined. Add it to the pan and whisk again.

Cook on medium low for about 4 minutes or until bubbles start to appear around the edge. Remove, add in the chocolate chips and whisk until well combined.

Lastly, divide between mugs and serve.

13. Almond Butter Hot Chocolate

A delicious hot drink with added nuttiness from almond butter.

Makes: 4 servings

Prep: 5 mins

Cook: 5 mins

Ingredients:

- 2 cups milk, divided
- 1 tbsp. chocolate syrup
- 2 tbsp. almond butter
- Whipped Cream

Directions:

In a saucepan, add the milk & heat until almost boiling. Add in the chocolate syrup and almond butter and mix till combined. Serve in mugs and add whipped cream on top.

14. Coconut Hot Chocolate

Hot chocolate made with coconut milk!

Makes: 4 servings

Prep: 5 mins

Cook: 5 mins

Ingredients:

- 2 cups coconut milk, divided
- 6 oz. semi-sweet chocolate
- 4 tbsp. cocoa powder
- ½ cup brown sugar
- 2 tsp. vanilla extract
- Pinch of salt

Directions:

First, in a large saucepan, combine milk, sugar and salt and cook for 4 mins/until sugar dissolves. Remove, add in the chocolate chips, cocoa and vanilla and whisk until well combined.

Lastly, divide between mugs and serve.

15. Candy Cane Hot Chocolate

This drink is perfect for festive seasons!

Makes: 4 servings

Prep: 5 mins

Cook: 5 mins

Ingredients:

- 2 cups milk, divided
- 1 cup heavy cream
- 1 ½ tsp. cornstarch
- 6 oz. white chocolate
- ¼ cup candy canes, crushed
- 1 ½ tsp. vanilla extract

Directions:

In a saucepan, combine 1 ½ cups milk and cream. In a bowl, whisk remaining milk and cornstarch until well combined. Add it to the pan and whisk again.

Cook on medium low for about 4 minutes or until bubbles start to appear around the edge. Remove, add in the chocolate, vanilla and candy canes and whisk until well combined.

Divide between mugs and serve.

16. KitKat Hot Chocolate

This one is loaded with KitKat!

Makes: 4 servings

Prep: 5 mins

Cook: 5 mins

Ingredients:

- 2 cups milk, divided
- 1 cup heavy cream
- 1 ½ tsp. cornstarch
- 6 oz. semi-sweet chocolate
- 4 KitKats, crushed, plus more for topping

Directions:

In a large saucepan, combine 1 ½ cups milk and cream. In a small bowl, whisk together remaining milk and cornstarch until well combined. Add it to the pan with the ground KitKat and whisk again.

Cook on medium low for about 4 minutes or until bubbles start to appear around the edge. Remove, add in the chocolate chips and whisk until well combined.

Divide between mugs and serve with KitKats on top.

17. Sea Salt Hot Chocolate

This hot chocolate has a hint of saltiness that makes it absolutely delicious!

Makes: 4 servings

Prep: 5 mins

Cook: 5 mins

Ingredients:

- 2 cups milk, divided
- 1 cup heavy cream
- 1 ½ tsp. cornstarch
- 6 oz. semi-sweet chocolate
- ½ tsp. sea salt

Directions:

In a large saucepan, combine 1 ½ cups milk and cream.

Next, in a small bowl, whisk together remaining milk and cornstarch until well combined. Add it to the pan and whisk again.

Cook on medium low for about 4 minutes or until bubbles start to appear around the edge. Remove, add in the chocolate chips and sea salt and whisk until well combined.

Lasty, divide between mugs and serve.

18. Cinnamon Hot Chocolate

Hot chocolate with a touch of cinnamon.

Makes: 4 servings

Prep: 5 mins

Cook: 5 mins

Ingredients:

- 2 cups milk, divided
- 3 tbsp. cocoa powder
- 1 tbsp. sugar
- 1/8 tsp. cinnamon
- 2 tbsp. chocolate chips

Directions:

In a large saucepan, combine milk, cocoa, sugar and cinnamon.

Cook on medium low for about 4 minutes or until bubbles start to appear around the edge. Remove, add in the chocolate chips and whisk until well combined.

Divide between mugs and serve.

19. White Mocha Hot Chocolate

A white chocolate and coffee-flavored hot chocolate recipe.

Makes: 4 servings

Prep: 5 mins

Cook: 5 mins

Ingredients:

- 2 cups milk, divided
- 1 cup heavy cream
- 1 ½ tsp. cornstarch
- 6 oz. white chocolate
- 1 ½ tsp. coffee powder

Directions:

In a large saucepan, combine 1 ½ cups milk and cream.

Next, in a small bowl, whisk together remaining milk and cornstarch until well combined. Add it to the pan and whisk again.

Cook on medium low for about 4 minutes or until bubbles start to appear around the edge. Remove, add in the chocolate and coffee powder and whisk until well combined.

Lastly, divide between mugs and serve.

20. Peanut Butter Mocha Hot Chocolate

What's better than peanut butter hot chocolate? This is peanut butter and mocha hot chocolate!

Makes: 4 servings

Prep: 5 mins

Cook: 5 mins

Ingredients:

- 2 cups milk, divided
- 1 tbsp. chocolate syrup
- 2 tbsp. peanut butter
- 2 tsp coffee powder
- Whipped cream

Directions:

In a saucepan, add the milk & heat until almost boiling. Add in the chocolate syrup, peanut butter, coffee powder and mix till combined. Serve in mugs and add whipped cream on top.

21. White Matcha Hot Chocolate

White chocolate with matcha? Yes, please!

Makes: 4 servings

Prep: 5 mins

Cook: 5 mins

Ingredients:

- 2 cups milk, divided
- 1 cup heavy cream
- 1 ½ tsp. cornstarch
- 6 oz. white chocolate
- 1 ½ tsp. vanilla extract
- 3 tsp. matcha powder

Directions:

In a large saucepan, combine 1 ½ cups milk and cream. In a small bowl, whisk together remaining milk and cornstarch until well combined. Add it to the pan and whisk again.

Cook on medium low for about 4 minutes or until bubbles start to appear around the edge. Remove, add in the chocolate, vanilla and matcha and whisk until well combined.

Divide between mugs and serve.

22. Double Chocolate Hot Chocolate

This is an intensely chocolatey hot chocolate recipe.

Makes: 4 servings

Prep: 5 mins

Cook: 5 mins

Ingredients:

- 2 cups milk, divided
- 1 cup heavy cream
- 1 ½ tsp. cornstarch
- 3 oz. dark chocolate chips
- 3 oz. milk chocolate chips

Directions:

In a large saucepan, combine 1 ½ cups milk and cream.

Next, in a small bowl, whisk together remaining milk and cornstarch until well combined. Add it to the pan and whisk again.

Cook on medium low for about 4 minutes or until bubbles start to appear around the edge. Remove, add in the chocolate chips and whisk until well combined.

Lastly, divide between mugs and serve.

23. Gingerbread Hot Chocolate

This drink is perfect for fall!

Makes: 8 servings

Prep: 5 mins

Cook: 5 mins

Ingredients:

- 8 cups milk
- ½ cup sugar
- 1 tsp. cinnamon
- 1/3 cup brown sugar
- 1 cup cocoa powder
- 1 tsp vanilla extract
- ½ tsp. sea salt
- 1 tsp. allspice
- 1 tsp. ground ginger
- 1/4 tsp. sea salt

Directions:

Heat the milk in a pan. In a bowl, mix the ingredients & then add it into the hot milk. Stir until combined. Serve.

24. Pumpkin Spice Hot Chocolate

This hot chocolate is amazing for colder months and around fall.

Makes: 4 servings

Prep: 5 mins

Cook: 5 mins

Ingredients:

- 2 cups milk, divided
- 1 cup heavy cream
- 1 ½ tsp. cornstarch
- 6 oz. semi-sweet chocolate
- 2 tsp. pumpkin puree
- 1 ½ tsp. pumpkin spice

Directions:

In a large saucepan, combine 1 ½ cups milk and cream.

Next, in a small bowl, whisk together remaining milk and cornstarch until well combined. Add it to the pan and whisk again.

Cook on medium low for about 4 minutes or until bubbles start to appear around the edge. Remove, add in the chocolate chips, pumpkin puree, pumpkin spice and whisk until well combined.

Lastly, divide between mugs and serve.

25. KitKat Mocha Hot Chocolate

KitKat hot chocolate with coffee!

Makes: 4 servings

Prep: 5 mins

Cook: 5 mins

Ingredients:

- 2 cups milk, divided
- 1 cup heavy cream
- 1 ½ tsp. cornstarch
- 2 tsp coffee powder
- 6 oz. semi-sweet chocolate
- 4 KitKats, crushed, plus more for topping

Directions:

In a large saucepan, combine 1 ½ cups milk and cream. In a small bowl, whisk together remaining milk and cornstarch until well combined. Add it along with the ground KitKat and whisk again.

Cook on medium low for about 4 minutes or until bubbles start to appear around the edge. Remove, add in the chocolate chips and coffee powder and whisk until well combined.

Divide between mugs and serve with KitKats on top.

26. Orange Mocha Hot Chocolate

Orange hot chocolate with an added bonus of mocha!

Makes: 4 servings

Prep: 5 mins

Cook: 5 mins

Ingredients:

- 2 cups milk, divided
- 1 cup heavy cream
- 1 ½ tsp. cornstarch
- Rind of an orange
- 2 tsp. instant coffee powder
- 6 oz. semi-sweet chocolate

Directions:

In a large saucepan, combine 1 ½ cups milk, cream and rind.

Next, in a small bowl, whisk together remaining milk and cornstarch until well combined. Add it to the pan and whisk again.

Cook on medium low for about 4 minutes or until bubbles start to appear around the edge. Remove and take out the rind. Add in the chocolate chips and whisk until well combined.

Lastly, divide between mugs and serve.

27. Vegan Hot Chocolate

If you are vegan, we have got you covered with this delicious hot chocolate recipe!

Makes: 4 servings

Prep: 5 mins

Cook: 5 mins

Ingredients:

- 4 cups almond milk, divided
- ¼ cup cocoa powder
- 1 tbsp. sugar
- 6 oz. dairy-free chocolate

Directions:

In a saucepan, mix the milk, cocoa powder and sugar.

Heat on low for a few minutes. Then, remove. Add in the chocolate and whisk until well combined.

Divide between mugs and serve.

28. Caramel Hot Chocolate

Delicious hot chocolate with caramel sauce and sea salt.

Makes: 4 servings

Prep: 5 mins

Cook: 5 mins

Ingredients:

- 2 cups milk, divided
- 1 cup heavy cream
- 1 ½ tsp. cornstarch
- 5 oz. semi-sweet chocolate
- ¼ cup caramel sauce, plus more for drizzling
- ½ tsp sea salt
- Whipped cream, for topping

Directions:

In a large saucepan, combine 1 ½ cups milk and cream. In a small bowl, whisk together remaining milk and cornstarch until well combined. Add it to the pan and whisk again.

Cook on medium low for about 4 minutes or until bubbles start to appear around the edge. Remove, add in the chocolate chips, caramel and sea salt and whisk until well combined.

Divide between mugs, top with whipped cream and caramel and serve.

29. Keto Hot Chocolate

If you are on a keto diet and still want to enjoy a delicious cup of hot chocolate, this recipe is for you!

Makes: 4 servings

Prep: 5 mins

Cook: 5 mins

Ingredients:

- ½ cup cocoa powder
- 3 tbsp. + 1 tsp keto-friendly sweetener
- 4 cups water
- 1 cup cream
- 1 tsp vanilla extract

Directions:

In a saucepan, combine ¼ cup water, cocoa and sweetener. Cook on low till sweetener is dissolved. Increase heat and then add in the remaining water and cream. Remove and add in vanilla.

Divide between mugs and serve.

30. Lavender White Hot Chocolate

The lavender perfectly complements the white chocolate in this recipe.

Makes: 4 servings

Prep: 5 mins

Cook: 5 mins

Ingredients:

- 2 cups milk, divided
- 1 cup heavy cream
- 1 tbsp. dried lavender
- 1 ½ tsp. cornstarch
- 6 oz. white chocolate
- 1 ½ tsp vanilla extract

Directions:

In a large saucepan, combine 1 ½ cups milk, cream and lavender.

Next, in a small bowl, whisk together remaining milk and cornstarch until well combined. Add it to the pan and whisk again.

Cook on medium low for about 4 minutes or until bubbles start to appear around the edge. Remove, add in the chocolate and vanilla and whisk until well combined.

Lastly, divide between mugs and serve.

Conclusion

There you have it! Delicious and warm hot chocolate recipes for you to enjoy during cozy cold months. Make sure you try out all the recipes in this book, and if you happen to love them, share them with your friends and family!

About the Author

A native of Indianapolis, Indiana, Valeria Ray found her passion for cooking while she was studying English Literature at Oakland City University. She decided to try a cooking course with her friends and the experience changed her forever. She enrolled at the Art Institute of Indiana which offered extensive courses in the culinary Arts. Once Ray dipped her toe in the cooking world, she never looked back.

When Valeria graduated, she worked in French restaurants in the Indianapolis area until she became the head chef at one of the 5-star establishments in the area. Valeria's attention to taste and visual detail caught the eye of a local business person who expressed an interest in publishing her recipes. Valeria began her secondary career authoring cookbooks and e-books which she tackled with as much talent and gusto as her first career. Her passion for food leaps off the page of her books which have colourful anecdotes and stunning pictures of dishes she has prepared herself.

Valeria Ray lives in Indianapolis with her husband of 15 years, Tom, her daughter, Isobel and their loveable Golden Retriever, Goldy. Valeria enjoys cooking special dishes in her large, comfortable kitchen where the family gets involved in preparing meals. This successful, dynamic chef is an inspiration to culinary students and novice cooks everywhere.

Author's Afterthoughts

Thank you for Purchasing my book and taking the time to read it from front to back. I am always grateful when a reader chooses my work and I hope you enjoyed it!

With the vast selection available online, I am touched that you chose to be purchasing my work and take valuable time out of your life to read it. My hope is that you feel you made the right decision.

I very much would like to know what you thought of the book. Please take the time to write an honest and informative review on Amazon.com. Your experience and opinions will be of great benefit to me and those readers looking to make an informed choice.

With much thanks,

Valeria Ray

Printed in Great Britain
by Amazon